A Fort for Kevin and Kate

By Sue Dickson and Vida Daly

Illustrated by Linda Finch

Vocabulary Words

1. be fore
   before

2. Core

3. corn

4. forks

5. fort

6. Forty

7. North

8. order

9. Or lan do
   Orlando

10. pork

11. Port

12. sore

13. sort

14. Sport

15. store

16. stork

17. torn

Story Words

18. begin

19. boxes

20. Brand

21. Chips

22. find

23. gave

24. good

   in side
25. inside

26. Kate

27. Kate's

28. Kevin

29. legs

30. list

   Mit tens
31. Mittens

32. Mom's

   (Mis ter)
33. Mr.

34. ones

35. paid

   pic nic
36. picnic

   plas tic
37. plastic

38. Pole

39. roast

40. too

41. want

"Let's make a fort for fun," said Kate.

"OK," said Kevin. "We will need some boxes. We must go to the store."

"Let's ask Mom if we may go," said Kate.

"Yes, you may go to the store," said Mom. "You can pick up my order. It is on this list. We need a pork roast, corn, and plastic forks for a picnic."

Kevin and Kate ran to the store. Kevin got Mom's order. Kate paid Mr. Orlando.

"Do you have any boxes?" asked Kate. "We need some."

"Yes," said Mr. Orlando, "but you will have to sort the boxes to find the ones you want. Some boxes are torn. They are all in the back of the store."

"Thank you!" said Kevin.

"I see a box," yelled Kate. "It has a big stork on it."

"Here is a big apple box," said Kevin.

"We can fit the little boxes inside the big ones," said Kate.

"We can get Mom's order in, too!" said Kevin.

"We have good boxes!" said Kevin. "What a fort we will have!"

"I am glad it is just a short way to North Street," said Kate. "My legs are getting sore."

At last, Kevin and Kate
got home! They gave
Mom her order and ran
to begin the fort.

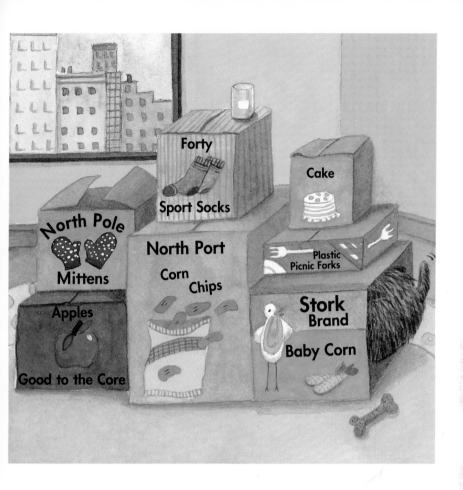

See Kevin and Kate's fort! What fun they will have! Seven boxes make a fine big fort!

The End

Sheldon's Bike Crash

By Vida Daly

Illustrated by Kristin Barr

Vocabulary Words

1. crash
2. crashed
3. crush
4. hush
5. polish
6. rush
7. Sheldon
8. Sheldon's
9. shin
10. shine
11. shorts
12. wish

Story Words

13. bandage
14. been
15. cleaned
16. driveway
17. giggled
18. gone
19. more
20. needs
21. path
22. rags
23. ripped
24. side
25. stone
26. tend

Sheldon left his bike by
the side of the driveway.
He hopped up the path
and held his shin.

"What did you do?"
asked Sheldon's mom.

"I fell off my bike," said
Sheldon. "I crashed when
I hit a stone."

"I was in a rush and
did not see the stone until
I hit it," said Sheldon.

"Did you crush your
hand?" asked Mom.

"No, I just hit my shin
and ripped my shorts,"
said Sheldon. "I wish I
had not gone so fast!"

"Hush," said Mom. "I wish you had not been in a crash, too, but you will be OK. Come sit in the shade and rest. I will tend to your shin."

Mom cleaned Sheldon's shin and then stuck a bandage on it.

Sheldon said, "Look at my bike, Mom. What a mess! It needs a bandage, too!"

"Some rags and polish will make it shine," said Mom.

Sheldon giggled. Mom was glad to see him happy once more.

The End

Cherry Hill Ranch

By Sue Dickson

Illustrated by Allan Eitzen

Vocabulary Words

1. bench
2. bunch
3. cheer ful
   cheerful
4. cheers
5. cheese
6. cherries
7. Cherry
8. chicken
9. chickens
10. child
11. children
12. chimes
13. chocolate
14. Chucky
15. Church
16. each
17. hunch
18. inch
19. lunch
20. march
21. munch
22. or chard
    orchard

23. punch

24. ranch

25. sand wich
    sandwich

26. sandwiches

27. scorch

28. such

29. teacher

30. teachers

Story Words

31. buddy

32. drink

33. Falls

34. hold

35. picks

36. reads

37. ring

38. sets

39. story

40. sum mer
    summer

24

Each year a bunch of children go to Cherry Hill Ranch. The ranch is near Church Falls. The children go with three teachers.

Each day the children
go to the chicken pen to
help feed the chickens.
Two chickens like to chase
the children. Next, the
children help pick peaches
or cherries from the trees
in the orchard.

The children eat lunch in the ranch hut. They sit on a bench. Not one inch of the bench is left to sit on! The children munch on big sandwiches with cheese. They drink cherry punch. Then, they have peach pie or chocolate cake.

After lunch, the children have rest time. At two o'clock, the chimes ring. Then, the children race to the beach at the pond.

"The hot sand will scorch your feet if you do not run fast!" yells Chucky.

28

The children then go
for a swim. Each child
picks a buddy to swim
with. It is safe to swim
when you have a buddy.

When the sun sets, the sand is not so hot. The children sit in a big bunch on the beach.

A teacher reads them the story: "Three Cheers for Summer." It is such a cheerful story.

Then, the children march up the hill. Off to bed they go.

Cherry Hill Ranch is such a fun place! Do you have a hunch the children will want to come back here each year?

The End

Cheer the Champ

By Vida Daly

Illustrated by Trevor Pye

Vocabulary Words

1. chain
2. champ
3. cheer
4. chest
5. Chet
6. chip
7. chisel
8. chose
9. much
10. porch
11. reach

Story Words

12. brush
13. care ful
    careful
14. drip
15. flash
16. hot rod
17. may be
    maybe
18. paint
19. press
20. shelf

"I would like to make
a hot rod," said Chet.
"I would like to race it in
the next Hot Rod Race."
"Fine," said Dad. "I will
help you."

Each day Dad and Chet
did more.

Dad said, "We need a
chain. Can you reach it,
Chet?"

"Yes, Dad," said Chet.

"I need my chisel to chip off one inch from this end," said Dad. "The chisel is in the chest."

"Yes, here it is," said Chet.

"May I paint my hot rod today, Dad?" asked Chet. "I would like to paint it red."

"I have some cherry red paint," said Dad. "It is on the shelf near the chest. Reach up to get it."

"I will teach you to paint," said Dad. "See me dip the brush in the can? I am careful to press it on each side so the paint will not drip."

"I can do it," said Chet.
"It is fun! I will not spill
or drip the paint. I will
make it a cherry red hot
rod," he said.

Mom came in from
the porch.

"Such a fine hot rod!"
she said. "I am glad you
chose cherry red. Maybe
you will be the champ!"
she said.

"I hope so," said Chet.

"I will name my hot rod Red Flash. I will be a champ with Red Flash. You must come to cheer the champ, Mom!" said Chet.

The End

A Shirt for Jenny

By Vida Daly

Illustrated by Ana Ochoa

Vocabulary Words

1. Bert

   bet ter
2. better

3. clerk

4. girl

5. grader

6. over

7. Shirley's

8. shirt

9. skirt

10. term

    Thurs day
11. Thursday

Story Words

12. dotted

13. grade

14. gray

15. Jenny

16. now

17. picked

    sea shore
18. seashore

19. Shelly

20. shop

The second-grade term
was over. Jenny waved
good-bye to her teacher.
Jenny, Bert, and Shelly
raced home.

"Mom! The term is over! I am a third grader now!" yelled Jenny. "May we go to the seashore?" she asked.

"Yes, we can go next Thursday," said Mom.

"Yippee!" cried Jenny. "I will need new shorts and a shirt."

"OK," said Mom. "Let's go to Shirley's shop on Third Street."

Jenny and her mom went to Shirley's store to shop.

"I need a new skirt. You need shorts and a shirt. We need a clerk to help us," said Mom.

A clerk came up to Jenny and her mom.

"I would like to try on the red shorts, the green ones, the gray ones, and the yellow shirt," said Jenny.

"Take one or two shorts, first," said the clerk. "You may try on some more after."

Jenny went to try on
the green shorts and the
yellow shirt.

"You look nice," said
Mom. "Here, try on the
blue dotted shirt and the
red shorts. You may like
the blue shirt and the red
shorts better."

In the end, Jenny picked the green shorts and the yellow shirt. Mom chose a pretty blue dress.

"I will pay you," said Mom to the clerk.

"This shirt will be fun at the seashore," smiled Jenny. "I can't wait to go!"

The End

Chocolate Dirt

By Vida Daly

Illustrated by Marion Eldridge

Vocabulary Words

1. bird
2. chirp
3. curved
4. dirt
5. Ervin
6. ever
7. fir
8. firm
9. germ
10. hurt
11. jerk
12. Miranda
13. sir
14. stir
15. swirls
16. thunder
17. turn

Story Words

18. asking
19. ended
20. I'll
21. pies
22. real
23. storm
24. tricked
25. tummy

"Look! The storm has ended," said Miranda. "The thunder and rain have stopped. Let's go, Ervin. We can make some mud pies!"

"First, we must fill up my purple pail with dirt and stir it," said Miranda. "Second, we must pack it till it is firm."

53

"Third, we will turn it over and lift up the pail," said Miranda.

"Try not to jerk it," said Ervin.

"Here, Ervin. You can make swirls on top. Use the curved stick," said Miranda.

"Look," said Ervin. "I see a bird. Did you hear it chirp in the fir tree? It is asking if our mud pie is real."

Miranda giggled. "We cannot let it eat the mud pie. The bird may get a germ! It would hurt its tummy!"

"No sir, a bird will not be tricked by our mud pies," said Ervin. "It is not so silly!"

"My tummy tells me it is lunch time," said Ervin. "I like chocolate dirt, but Mom's lunch is better! I'll race you inside, Miranda!" Off they went!

The End

Chipper Gets Hurt

By Vida Daly

Illustrated by Winifred Barnum-Newman

Vocabulary Words

1. burst
2. curb
3. curl
4. Curly
5. fur
6. hurry
7. Kurt
8. urge

Story Words

9. care
10. Chipper

11. dog
12. flying
13. kicked
14. loves
15. mas ter
    master
16. on to
    onto
17. places
18. tried
19. tripped

Chipper was a little
black dog who had the
urge to see new places.
So, one day he left home.

On the way, he met a big dog with brown and white fur. His tail had a big curl in it.

"May I go with you?" asked Chipper.

"OK," said the big dog. "My name is Curly. We will visit my dog pals."

"Let's turn onto North Street," said Curly.

Just then some children kicked a ball. It burst onto the road and came flying at Chipper and Curly.

"Hurry," yelled Curly, "or you will get hit and get hurt!"

Chipper ran. He tried to jump up on the curb, but he tripped. The ball hit him.

"Curly! Curly!" he yelled. "I hurt my leg. I must go home," said Chipper.

"My master, Kurt, will take care of me. He loves me."

Chipper went home to Kurt as fast as he could!

The End